• T R O P H I E S •

Intervention
PRACTICE BOOK
Grade 2

Harcourt

Orlando   Boston   Dallas   Chicago   San Diego

Visit The Learning Site!
www.harcourtschool.com

Printed in the United States of America

ISBN 0-15-326145-5

3 4 5 6 7 8 9 10 054 10 09 08 07 06 05 04 03

Table of Contents

Fluency Builder

dull	things	Mac
exciting	see	animals
handsome	look	wap
hardly	wait	zap
sideways		fan
sparkling		that
spotted		had
		sad
		bad

1. Mac thought / things were dull.

2. He wanted to go / to the zoo / to see the exciting animals.

3. Mac saw / two spotted / and handsome animals / at the zoo.

4. They could look sideways / with their long necks.

5. Mac wished / he could look / like the animal / that had a sparkling fan.

6. Wap! / Zap! / Mac's wish / came true.

7. Mac could hardly wait / to show his pals / how handsome he was.

8. Mac was sad / and felt bad / when he had no pals.

Mac's Wish Comes True

Write the word from the box that best completes each sentence.

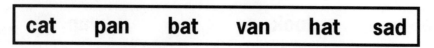

cat	pan	bat	van	hat	sad

1. My _____ is in my lap.

2. The jam is in the _____.

3. Pam has on a _____.

4. This man is not _____.

5. That _____ had a nap.

6. A cat is in that _____!

Harcourt

Mac's Wish Comes True

Complete the flowchart with words from the box to tell what happens in "Mac's Wish Comes True."

dull	zoo	pals	true	wish	hungry

Mac sat with his _____.

"This is _____," he said.

Mac went to the _____.

Mac saw two _____ animals there.

"I _____ I was handsome," Mac said.

His wish did come _____.

Write the answers to these questions to tell the rest of the story.

1. What did Mac wish for next? _____

_____

2. What did the animals in the river ask Mac when he got home?

_____

3. What did you like best in this story?

_____

_____

Main Idea

Write three clues that tell about the main idea of the paragraph. Then write the main idea.

Pat the ant wished he looked like something else. One day Pat wished he was a bird. Pat's wish came true, but he did not know how to use his new wings. Next, Pat wished he was a cat, and his wish came true. Then a big dog came along. Pat was afraid, so he wished he was a fish. Pat's wish came true, but then a fisherman tried to catch him. Finally, Pat wished he could be an ant again, and his wish came true. Looking like an ant was not so bad!

Clue:

Clue:

Clue:

Main Idea:

Harcourt

Fluency Builder

always	get	Stan
homework	does	Fran
minutes	must	stands
snuggle	what	add
treat	coming	black
	company	grab
	trip	glad
		Brad

1. Fran always / does her homework, / while Brad / eats a treat.

2. Fran wants / to add black / to her map.

3. In just ten minutes, / Stan must / get off the mat.

4. Cass wants to snuggle /with her cat, / but there is no more time.

5. Dad tells the children / to stop / what they are doing.

6. Stan is glad / that company is coming, / but Dad is the one / that has to grab / all the toys.

7. Dad picks up / all the toys / so that the company / will not trip / on them.

8. In the end, / the family stands together / to wait / for their company.

Harcourt

Company Is Coming!

Read the story. Circle all the words that begin with two consonants.

Stan has a cat and a flag. Fran has a hat. Stan and Fran skip.

Stan trips. He drops his cat and his flag. Fran has a plan.

Fran grabs her hat. Fran grabs his cat. Fran grabs his flag.

Stan is glad. His cat is glad. Stan and his cat like Fran.

Write the word that best completes each sentence.

1. Stan has a cat and a _____ .

   flag   skip   plan

2. _____ has a hat.

   Cat   Fran   Stan

3. Stan _____ the flag.

   skips   plans   drops

4. Fran _____ the cat and the flag.

   grabs   skips   drops

5. Stan and the cat are _____ .

   clams   glad   small

Harcourt

Company Is Coming!

Read the story. Then fill in the chart with details about the family.

Dad wanted everyone to get ready because company was coming to visit. Little Brad was not ready because he was eating a treat. Fran was not ready because she was doing her homework. Cass was not ready because she was playing with the cat. Stan was not ready because he was on the mat. Finally, everyone was ready, but then Dad was missing. He was taking a nap just when company came to the door.

Why isn't Brad ready?	Why isn't Fran ready?

Why isn't Cass ready?	Why isn't Stan ready?

Harcourt

Name _____

Author's Purpose

Write the author's purpose. Then write three clues that helped you tell the author's purpose.

Company was coming to Fred Frog's house. "Get ready," Fred Frog called to his froggy brothers. "Company is coming in ten minutes!"

None of Fred Frog's froggy brothers were ready. They were all busy playing baseball, sailing boats, and eating pizza. "Please help me clean up all these lily pads!" called Fred Frog. "Company is coming in five minutes!"

Author's Purpose:

Clue:

Clue:

Clue:

Fluency Builder

chipmunks	down	Kim
picked	fall	Tip
sniffing	few	bit
south	apples	did
woods	trees	will
	could	zip
	go	sit
	were	

1. Kim and Tip / loved to go / for walks / in the woods.

2. Kim / loved walking / in the fall leaves.

3. Tip loved / sniffing the fall leaves.

4. Kim picked / a few apples, / and her dog / looked for chipmunks.

5. The apple trees / were south / of the woods.

6. Kim and Tip / will sit / for a bit.

7. They will see / a chipmunk / zip up the tree.

8. They could see / the chipmunk, / but it did not / come down.

Harcourt

A Walk in the Woods

Fill in the oval in front of the sentence that tells about the picture.

1 ⬭ My cat hid in the tin.
   ⬭ Tim did find his bat.
   ⬭ The cat sits in his lap.

2 ⬭ She is sitting with her bat.
   ⬭ She is sitting in a van.
   ⬭ She is hitting now.

3 ⬭ Is that a pig in the van?
   ⬭ That pig is so big!
   ⬭ I see a pig in a wig.

4 ⬭ Tim finds a pin in the bin.
   ⬭ Is the wig in the bin?
   ⬭ All my hats are in the bin.

5 ⬭ She did win a bat.
   ⬭ She did win a pin.
   ⬭ She is in the van.

6 ⬭ This fits him.
   ⬭ This is big for him.
   ⬭ He is sitting down.

Harcourt

Name _____

A Walk in the Woods

Complete the story strip to show what happened in "A Walk in the Woods."

When do Kim and Tip like to go for walks? _____ _____	Where do Kim and Tip like to go for walks? _____ _____
Who loves sniffing the leaves? _____ _____	Who loves the apples in the trees? _____ _____
What animal do Kim and Tip see? _____ _____	What if you could go for a walk in the woods. What would you like to see there? _____ _____ _____

Harcourt

Narrative Elements (Setting)

Write the setting of the paragraph. Write two clues that tell when and two clues that tell where.

One hundred years ago, a boy named Max lived in a treehouse in a very tall tree. The very tall tree grew in a forest called Big Green Forest. One summer day, Max's dog, Kip, woke him up. Max and Kip heard a funny sound coming from the roof of the treehouse.

Setting: _____	
_____	
Clue That Tells When: _____ _____	**Clue That Tells When:** _____ _____
Clue That Tells Where: _____ _____	**Clue That Tells Where:** _____ _____

Harcourt

Fluency Builder

alone	fun	call
cheer	right	all
fine	made	wall
meadow	think	tall
reason	play	mall
spoiled	when	ball
	friends	fine

1. Hal sat / alone at home, / but he did not think / it was fun.

2. He made a call, / and asked Rip / to cheer him up.

3. Rip's nap / was spoiled, / but he felt / all right.

4. Mack is digging / in the meadow / when Hal calls.

5. Hal / had no reason / to be alone.

6. The friends / could all / play ball.

7. It was a fine day / to go to the river, / or visit the mall.

8. Hal sat / next to the tall wall / as he made his call.

Harcourt

One Fine Night

Write the word that makes the sentence tell about the picture.

1. It is _____.

   fall   **fan**   **for**

2. Kim and her dad are at the

   _____.

   make   **mall**   **man**

3. They go down a big _____.

   pal   **have**   **hall**

4. "Look over this _____, Kim."

   will   **wall**   **wax**

5. Kim is not _____.

   tall   **that**   **tap**

6. "Look at _____ the cats!"

   are   **and**   **all**

7. "Can I have the one with the _____?"

   ban   **bat**   **ball**

8. "We will _____ Mom."

   come   **call**   **can**

Harcourt

One Fine Night

Fill in the story map to tell about "One Fine Night." Use the words in the gray boxes.

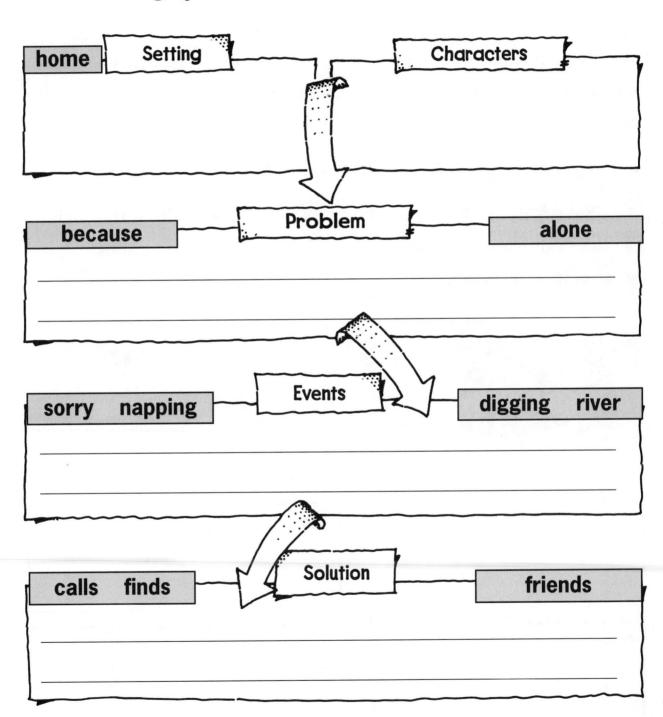

home | Setting

Characters

because | Problem | alone

sorry | napping | Events | digging | river

calls | finds | Solution | friends

Harcourt

Name_____

Compare and Contrast

Read the two stories. Compare and contrast the characters.

Pal's Fine Night

Pal sits in his dog house. He is happy being alone. It is a very fine night to look at the stars and think about how lucky he is to be a dog. Pal is very glad that he has such a big dog house.

Sal's Lonely Night

Sal sits in his dog house. He is lonely. He is afraid of the dark. He does not like to look at the stars. Sal is sad in his dog house because it is too small.

Characters:	Alike:
Different:	

Fluency Builder

amazing	ball	Bob
clustered	but	pot
gathered	snow	mop
raced	watch	hop
wandered	look	hot
	friend	not
	groups	
	one	
	after	

1. The children clustered / in groups, / but I did not.

2. I gathered snow / and made one ball / after another.

3. Bob / was amazing, / but he could not / get hot.

4. Each time / I raced, / Bob would / watch me.

5. I wandered alone / to look / for a pot / and a mop.

6. Bob would watch / me hop.

7. A snow friend / cannot be there / when it is hot.

8. Do you want / to know / the name / of my snow friend?

Harcourt

Just You and Me

Read the story. Circle all the words with the short *o* vowel sound.

Mom has a pot. Bob has the top.

Bob fills the pot. Mom makes it hot.

Bob has a mop. Mom looks in the pot.

Mom makes lots of jam. Bob is not sad!

Circle the word to complete each sentence. Write it on the line.

1. Mom got the _____.

                pit   pot   pat

2. Bob got a _____ for the pot.

                tap   tip   top

3. Mom made the pot _____.

                hit   hat   hot

4. Bob had to get the _____.

                mop   man   mad

5. Bob likes jam a _____!

                lid   lap   lot

Harcourt

Name _____

Just You and Me

Write *beginning*, *middle*, **or** *end* **to show when each thing happened.**

_____   _____   _____

Now write what happened in the story. Use the words in the boxes in your answers.

Beginning:		school played friends

_____

_____

Middle:		snow loved Bob

_____

_____

End:		friends desk

_____

_____

Narrative Elements (Character)

Read the story. Fill in the chart with a character. Then write clues from the story that tell about the character.

Mara's Play Pal

Mara sat alone on her front steps and watched the other children play. Everyone had a play pal except her. All of a sudden, a little white cat came to sit next to her. "I am lonely, little kitty," said Mara. "Will you play with me?" The cat rubbed against Mara's arm and purred. Mara smiled. For the rest of the day, Mara played with the cat.

Character:	Word Clues:

Action Clues:

Harcourt

Fluency Builder

enormous	hill	get
granddaughter	some	men
grew	help	fell
planted	well	best
strong	mouse	then
turnip	woman	bent
		rest
		mess

1. A woman / planted a turnip / on a hill.

2. The turnip / grew to be / enormous.

3. The turnip / fell into the well / and made a mess.

4. The woman / called / her granddaughter / to help.

5. They pulled, / but they could not get / the turnip / out of the well.

6. Some strong men / came to help, / but they could not pull / the turnip / from the well.

7. Then / a mouse said, / "I can help."

8. The mouse / bent over / the well / and did his best.

9. The rest helped, / and they pulled / the turnip / out at last.

A Turnip's Tale

Write the word that best completes each sentence.

wet	nest	bell	ten	bed	sled	men

1. Two _____ go to the zoo.

2. The cat is on the _____ .

3. Can you see the _____ ?

4. Her _____ can go down.

5. The _____ is in the tree.

6. These animals are _____ .

7. There are _____ red apples.

Harcourt

A Turnip's Tale

These events are from "A Turnip's Tale." They are out of order. Write a number in front of each one to show the right order.

_____ A mouse came to help.

_____ The granddaughter asked some men to help.

_____ The turnip fell into a well.

_____ They all pulled, but they could not get the turnip out.

_____ The woman called her granddaughter.

Now write each event in the order it happened. Put each one next to an X. Then write other story events on the blank lines.

X _____

X _____

X _____

X _____

X _____

_____

_____

_____

Sequence

These sentences are not in time order.

The carrot grew to be enormous.

After it grew, the enormous carrot rolled down the hill.

First, an old woman planted a carrot on a hill.

Finally, the carrot rolled into the pond.

Write the sentences in correct order to complete the diagram.

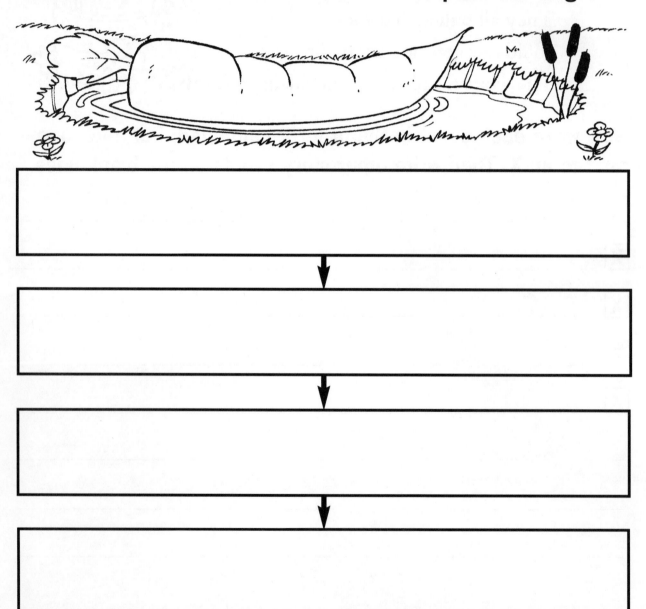

Harcourt

Fluency Builder

alongside	used	wish
chores	what	dishes
engine	fix	Tish
simple	help	Shep
sprout	flowers	brush
tool	thinks	wash
	paint	shop

1. Ted likes digging / with a tool / alongside his mom.

2. Ted makes a wish / that the plants / will sprout / pretty flowers.

3. Doing the dishes / is Jim's chore.

4. Jim thinks / it is simple / to wash the plates.

5. Tish helps / her dad / fix an engine / in the shop.

6. Ben used / a paint brush / to help paint / the fence.

7. Pat thinks / walking Shep / is like playing.

8. What chores / do you do?

Tools That Help

Fill in the oval in front of the sentence that tells about the picture.

1 ⬭ Ben hands her his cash.
⬭ Ben makes a dash to the shed.
⬭ Ben makes a wish.

2 ⬭ Tad looks at the big ship.
⬭ Tad has a pet fish.
⬭ Tad has lost his dish.

3 ⬭ Jen drops the dish.
⬭ Jen sees a red fish.
⬭ Jen is on a ship.

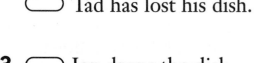

4 ⬭ The shed fell over.
⬭ I see a hen on the ship.
⬭ The hen is in the shed.

5 ⬭ The cat has a fish.
⬭ The cat sits by the shop.
⬭ Now a cat is in the shack!

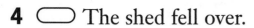

6 ⬭ They wish they had a ball and bat.
⬭ They find a shell.
⬭ They make a dash for the bus.

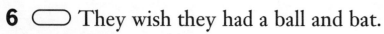

Harcourt

Tools That Help

Complete the puzzle by using words from the box.

| digging | learning | job | paid | helping | tools | chore |

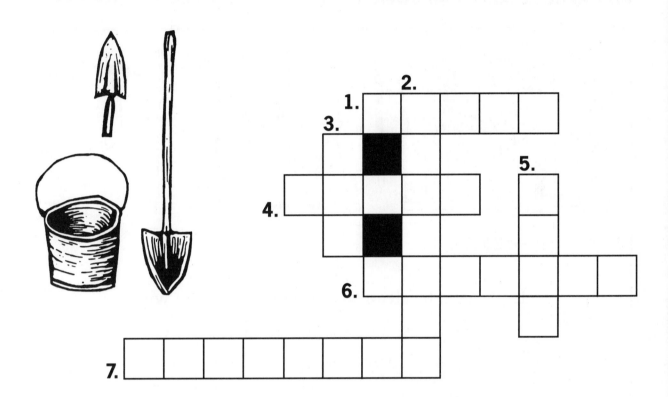

Across

1. Pat's _____ is walking her dog.

4. Some kids used _____ to help with the jobs.

6. Ted likes _____ with his mom.

7. Tish is _____ as she works.

Down

2. Jim likes _____ out at home.

3. Tish said that fixing an engine is a _____ for an adult.

5. Jim is not _____ for washing the dishes.

Harcourt

Main Idea

This paragraph has a main idea and other ideas that tell more about the main idea. Identify the main idea of the paragraph, and write it on the line below.

Leah likes to clean the garage. First, she wipes off the garden tools. Then, she puts them away. The last thing she does is sweep the floor.

Main Idea _____

_____

Harcourt

Fluency Builder

cranes	this	Lun
directions	here	Crump
promise	some	dug
twitch	toy	but
worry	shop	Bud
		Muffin
		sun
		hum
		bug
		rug

1. "Mr. Crump, / will that plane / run?" / asked Lun.

2. "No, / but this / plane will," / said Mr. Crump.

3. "Here are / the directions," / said Mr. Crump.

4. Bud looked / at some cranes / in the toy shop.

5. Mr. Crump's cat, / Muffin, / was sitting / in the sun.

6. Muffin twitched / when she heard / the hum / of a bug.

7. Muffin dug / in the rug / for the bug.

8. Mr. Crump said, / "Do not worry, / because I promise / that Muffin will get the bug."

Harcourt

The Promise

Read the sentences. Look at the picture. Then do what the sentences tell you.

1. Ned has a jug. Make it red.

2. Draw a cup for Ned.

3. Find the plums. Draw an apple to go with the plums.

4. Draw the sun over the trees.

5. Draw a red bug on a tree.

6. A pup runs to Ned. Make it black.

7. Find the animal that likes nuts. Draw some nuts for it.

Now circle the words in the sentences that have the short _u_ sound.

Harcourt

The Promise

Read the sentences. Choose and write the word to complete each one. Use the words to retell the first part of the story.

1. Lun asks Mr. Crump if the

_____

    bug   plane   cat

will go.

2. Lun and his mom

_____

    lost   bent   bought

the toy.

3. Bud asks Mr. Crump if
the crane will

_____.

    start   lift   stop

4. Muffin is Mr. Crump's

_____.

    bug   toy   cat

Use words from the box to answer these questions. Write your answers on the lines to retell the rest of the story.

toys	bug	fly

5. What did Bud's dad say a bug can do? _____

6. What spilled over in the shop when Muffin jumped at the

bug? _____

7. What did Muffin see at the end of the story? _____

Harcourt

Name _____

Predict Outcomes

The ending of this paragraph is missing. Look for clues. Then predict what will happen next.

Mr. Tibbit fell asleep in the chair. His cat, Blackie, sat in his lap. Suddenly, Mr. Tibbit let out a loud snore. Blackie jerked and fell out of the chair. He woke up Mr. Tibbit. Blackie crawled back in Mr. Tibbit's lap. Mr. Tibbit fell asleep. Suddenly, Mr. Tibbit let out a loud snore. _____.

Write the clues you used to make your prediction. Draw a picture to show what you predict will happen next.

Clues   Predicted Outcome

Harcourt

Fluency Builder

batter	**went**	**think**
buttery	**cake**	**whiz**
perfect	**put**	**thud**
recipe	**smell**	**thump**
smeared	**fell**	**wham**
yellow cake	**began**	**what**
		bathtub
		thick

1. Possum said, / "I think cupcakes / are grand."

2. Rabbit / was a whiz / in the kitchen.

3. He had a recipe / for a buttery / yellow cake.

4. Possum dropped the bowl, / and it went thud, / thump, / and wham!

5. "What can we put / our cake batter in now?" / asked Possum.

6. Rabbit said, / "It will be perfect / to put / the thick batter / into the bathtub."

7. Possum fell in the tub / and was smeared / with batter.

8. Rabbit put / the cupcakes / into the open oven, / and soon the kitchen / began to smell good.

Harcourt

Too Many Cupcakes

Read the story. Circle all the words with *wh* or *th*.

Seth Makes Broth

Seth makes broth. He wants his broth to be thick. Now Seth has some broth. It is not thick. It is thin!

Seth whips up an egg. He adds the egg to his broth. Now his broth is thick. Seth is glad.

Circle and write the word that best completes each sentence.

1. Seth makes _____.

          whip   broth   path

2. Seth likes _____ broth.

       bath   when   thick

3. The broth Seth makes is _____.

             tin   thin   with

4. Seth _____ an egg.

    whips   with   wishes

5. Now the broth is _____.

       thick   both   when

Harcourt

Too Many Cupcakes

Answer the questions below to tell about "Too Many Cupcakes."

1. Who was a whiz in the kitchen, Possum or Rabbit? _____	**2.** Who let the bowl land with a crash? _____
3. What did Rabbit and Possum mix in the bathtub? _____	**4.** Who fell into the bathtub? _____
5. How did the hot oven help Possum? _____ _____	**6.** What can Possum do with the cupcakes? _____ _____

What do you like best in the story?

_____

_____

_____

_____

Harcourt

Synonyms

Read each sentence. Find the synonym for the underlined word. Write it on the line above the underlined word.

1. Robin was building a new <u>home</u> in the apple tree.

   school   house   library

2. Robin used many small <u>twigs</u> to make a nest.

   sticks   stones   nuts

3. "What can I use to <u>hold</u> the twigs together?" Robin wondered.

   move   keep   push

Reread each sentence with your word choice to make sure the sentence makes sense.

Harcourt

Fluency Builder

announced	some	Barb
arrived	enough	yard
glum	fell	Mark
members	idea	Karl
rebuild	number	started
	because	card
	stand	are
	said	

1. Barb / was glum / because she missed / her friends.

2. She took / some lemonade / to the kids / in the next yard.

3. Their clubhouse fell down, / and they didn't have / enough money / to rebuild it.

4. Karl had the idea / to sell lemonade / to earn money.

5. A large number / of people arrived / to buy lemonade.

6. When they closed the stand, / Mark announced / that they had enough money.

7. A card / on the clubhouse door / said / "Just Members."

8. Barb started to leave, / but Karl said, / "You are a friend, / and that makes you a member."

Harcourt

A Lemonade Surprise

Circle the word that makes the sentence tell about the picture.
Then write the word.

1. "It is time to go. Let's get into the

_____ ," said Mom.

      barn   car   cat

2. We got a snack at the

_____ .

    farm   barn   market

3. It was not _____

         far   yard   fat

to the park.

4. I got up on the _____ .

         bars   jars   harm

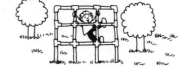

5. It was _____

        had   hard   tar

to find Mark when he hid.

6. We left the park when it got

_____ .

    wet   dark   cart

7. We had fun at the _____ !

      park   farm   pack

Harcourt

A Lemonade Surprise

Read the clues. Then complete the puzzle with words from the box.

clubhouse	empty	sales	wrong	money

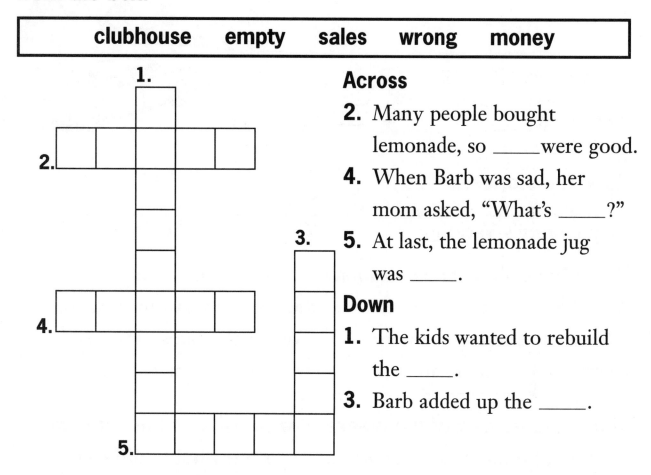

Across

2. Many people bought lemonade, so _____ were good.

4. When Barb was sad, her mom asked, "What's _____?"

5. At last, the lemonade jug was _____.

Down

1. The kids wanted to rebuild the _____.

3. Barb added up the _____.

Write what you liked best about the story. Use as many words from the box as you can.

_____

_____

_____

_____

Harcourt

Name _____

Compare and Contrast

Read the stories.

My Family's Vacation	Our Trip to the East
My family went on vacation out West. We saw mountains. We saw the desert. We went swimming in the ocean.	My family went east on vacation. We saw mountains. We saw the forest. We went swimming in the ocean.

In the middle part of the diagram, write what is the same in the two stories. In the outside parts, write what is different.

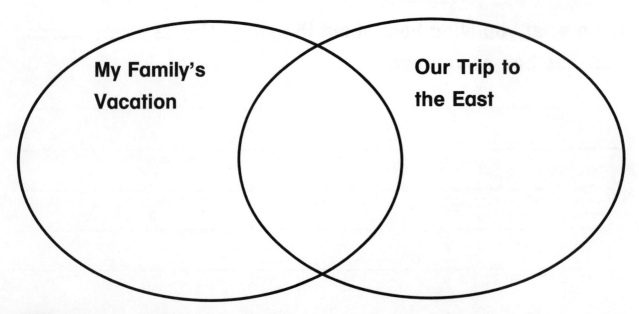

Harcourt

Fluency Builder

frontier	**down**	**batch**
nearby	**fish**	**Charles**
orchards	**country**	**ditch**
survive	**must**	**chop**
tame	**rain**	**catch**
wild	**tree**	**watch**
		stitch
		Mitch

1. You must tame / a wild animal / to survive / on the frontier.

2. Mitch / can catch fish / in the rain.

3. Anna / will pick apples / in the orchard nearby.

4. Anna / likes / the country.

5. Charles /will chop down / a tree.

6. Garth picks / a batch of apples / and puts them / in a basket.

7. Watch out / so you don't fall / into the ditch!

8. Mom will stitch the dress / before going / to sleep.

Harcourt

Name _____

Anna's Apple Doll

Fill in the oval in front of the sentence that tells about the picture.

1 ⬭ The chick has an itch on its chest.
 ⬭ The cat has an itch on its chin.
 ⬭ The cat has an itch on its back.

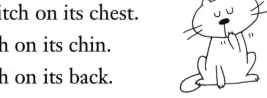

2 ⬭ Dan can stitch the patch.
 ⬭ Dan can catch a fast pitch.
 ⬭ We will switch the chart.

3 ⬭ Mitch is catching a fish.
 ⬭ Anna can pitch fast.
 ⬭ Anna is catching that ball.

4 ⬭ Ben and Sam chat by the ditch.
 ⬭ Ben and Sam pitch in the kitchen.
 ⬭ Ben and Sam chat in the kitchen.

5 ⬭ Chen and Pat have matching patches.
 ⬭ Chen and Pat have matching charms.
 ⬭ Chen and Pat have matching charts.

6 ⬭ Mitch is stitching a patch.
 ⬭ Mitch is catching a pitch.
 ⬭ Mitch is switching his hat.

Harcourt

Name_____

Anna's Apple Doll

Think about what happened in "Anna's Apple Doll."
Write about the *beginning*, *middle*, and *end* of the
play. Use the words from the boxes in your answers.

Beginning		**cabin west**

Where does the play happen?

_____

_____

What does Anna's mom ask her to do?   **outdoors   apples**

_____

_____

Middle		**seeds sticks**

What does Anna use to make her doll?

_____

_____

End		**cabin family**

Where does Anna take her doll? What happens there?

_____

_____

Harcourt

Details

**Read the paragraph carefully. Find the
details that tell about the topic.**

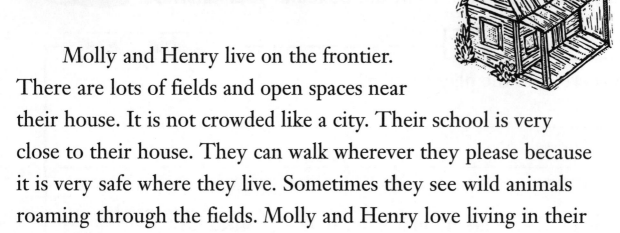

Molly and Henry live on the frontier.
There are lots of fields and open spaces near
their house. It is not crowded like a city. Their school is very
close to their house. They can walk wherever they please because
it is very safe where they live. Sometimes they see wild animals
roaming through the fields. Molly and Henry love living in their
frontier home.

Topic: Frontier

Detail: _____

Detail: _____

Detail: _____

Detail: _____

Detail: _____

Harcourt

Fluency Builder

beautiful	air	forming
nutrition	different	short
protects	flowers	for
ripens	grow	corn
streams	past	thorns
	plant	horses
	seed	
	tall	
	the	

1. The sunflowers / in the garden / will grow tall.

2. Water from the streams, / together with air and light, / will help the seeds / become flowers.

3. The seed / travels past the thorns / and the horses.

4. The pod ripens / and becomes corn.

5. There are seeds forming / on the pod.

6. The pod protects / the seeds.

7. Leaves make nutrition / for the plant.

8. Different kinds of flowers / are grown / in the garden.

Harcourt

A Day in the Life of a Seed

Look at the picture. Then do what the sentences tell you.

1. Bob, Cora, and Tim are on the team in the red shorts. Make their shorts red.

2. Peg, Mort, and Greg are on the team in the black shorts. Make Greg's shorts black.

3. Tim wants to score more runs. Give him a bat.

4. The team in the red shorts scored four runs. Put a four in the score box.

5. Greg is not playing the right sport. Put an X on his club.

Now circle the words above that have *or*, *ore*, and *our*.

Harcourt

A Day in the Life of a Seed

Complete the sentences with words from the box to tell what happens in "A Day in the Life of a Seed."

sprout	plant	soil	flowers	roots

1. The garden has lots of tall, yellow _____.

2. A rabbit pulls up grass. The seed falls to the _____.

3. The seed will start to _____.

4. First, _____ will form and go down into the soil.

5. Soon it becomes a tall _____.

Write what you liked best about the story. Use as many words from the box as you can.

_____

_____

_____

_____

Reading Diagrams

Read the diagram. Then use the labels to fill in the blanks.

1. This is the outside of the watermelon. _____.

2. These are found inside the watermelon. _____.

3. This is attached to the watermelon. _____.

4. The vine grows out of this. _____.

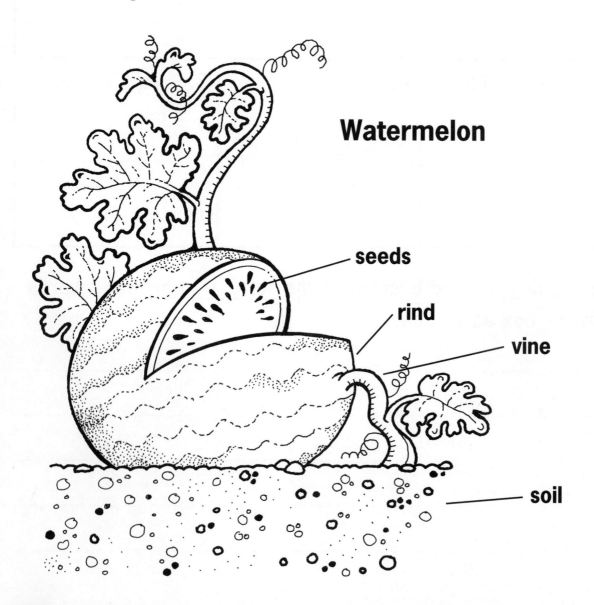

Watermelon

seeds

rind

vine

soil

Harcourt

Fluency Builder

discover	tree	her
energy	sun	weather
forecast	winds	uncurl
shed	winter	birds
source	bark	chirp
	little	perfect
	rabbit	turn
	family	

1. All summer, / the tree's leaves / take energy from the sun.

2. The cold winds / forecast winter weather.

3. Birds discover / the bugs / on the bark / of the tree.

4. The birds chirp and sleep / in the branches / of the tree.

5. In the spring / new little leaves uncurl / and turn / to the sun.

6. The log is / the perfect spot / for the mother rabbit / and her family.

7. The tree will shed / its bark.

8. A tree is / a source of life / to many living things.

Name _____

The Old Tree

Read the story. Circle the words with *er*, *ir*, or *ur*.

A bird and a turtle met one day. "I can surf!" the turtle said.

"Well, I can fly," said the bird. "Let's go up to my perch."

"Let's go surfing," said the turtle. "No thanks," said the bird. "I do not want to surf. I will get my shirt wet."

"As you like," said the turtle. "Now, will you get me back on firm ground? This perch is too far up for a turtle."

Circle the word to complete each sentence. Write it on the line.

1. A _____ and a turtle met one day.
third   bird   perfect

2. The bird took the turtle to its _____ .
surf   perch   turn

3. The bird did not want to get its _____ wet.
shirt   perch   dirt

4. The turtle wanted to get back on _____ ground.
firm   term   first

Harcourt

The Old Tree

Fill in the first two parts of the chart before you read the story.

What I Know	What I Want to Know	What I Learned

After you read, answer these questions. Then, in the third part of the chart, write new facts you learned.

1. What happens to the bark on a tree as it grows older and

   weaker? _____

2. How do animals use dead tree parts such as empty logs?

   _____

3. What living thing can grow on a log?

   _____

Harcourt

Fact and Fiction

Read the description of each book. Look carefully at each book title on the book cover. Write *Fact* or *Fiction* on the lines.

_____

This book gives step-by-step directions for building the perfect campfire.

_____

This book tells how a family of bunnies plans a surprise party for their best friend.

_____

This book tells all about a second grade field trip to pick apples in an orchard. It includes photos.

Harcourt

Fluency Builder

beneath	**look**	**sounds**
knelt	**all**	**ground**
relay race	**were**	**down**
shimmered	**over**	**sprouts**
snug	**good**	**now**
wrinkled	**made**	**proud**
		pounded
		tower

1. Mr. Carver and Ben / were wrinkled all over.

2. The seeds / were snug / in the soil.

3. Ben / knelt down / on the ground / to look at the sprouts.

4. The sun / pounded down / on the sprouts.

5. The carrot sprouts shimmered / in the heat.

6. Ben made a tower / of carrots.

7. They / were very proud / of their garden.

8. Now / watermelon sounds good / to Ben and Mr. Carver.

Mr. Carver's Carrots

Read the story. Circle all the words with the vowel sound you hear in *cow* and *found*.

At the Farm

Beth has a farm. Color her barn red. Color her house brown. Beth has four cows and a cat called Clown. Clown likes to run around.

Now Beth is plowing the ground. Clown has found a mouse. The mouse is about to fall down!

Now write a word with *ou* or *ow* to complete each sentence.

1. Beth's house is _____.

2. Beth has a cat and four _____.

3. Now Beth is plowing the _____.

4. The cat has _____ a mouse.

5. The mouse is about to fall _____.

Harcourt

Name _____

Mr. Carver's Carrots

These events are from "Mr. Carver's Carrots." They are out of order. Put a number in front of each one to show the right order.

_____ Mr. Carver and Ben munched on carrots.

_____ Sprouts came up after a storm.

_____ Mr. Carver and Ben pulled the carrots out of the ground.

_____ Ben put carrot seeds under the soil.

Now write the events in order. Put each one next to its number.

1. _____

_____

2. _____

_____

3. _____

_____

4. _____

_____

Make Inferences

Read the paragraph. Complete the sentence to make an inference. Write three clues that helped you make the inference.

    Tom's alarm clock rang at 6 A.M. He jumped out of bed and dressed. He went to the back door, put on his rubber boots, and grabbed the milk pail. He could hear the cows in the barn. "I'm coming! I'm coming!" he called as he ran toward the barn.

Inference: Tom is going to

Clue:

Clue:

Clue:

Fluency Builder

boasted	rabbit	shame
crept	fox	ate
crown	mouse	late
village	into	rake
vines	many	spade
	work	gate
	again	came
	from	

1. Miss Owl wins / the village's Best Melon Contest / all the time.

2. It's a shame / the leaves are small / and withered / on the tangled vines.

3. Kit Fox, / Pocket Mouse, / and Jack Rabbit / met at the gate / and crept / into the garden.

4. With a spade and a rake / they worked late.

5. They came / many evenings / to work in the garden.

6. "This is my best crop / ever," / boasted Miss Owl.

7. Everyone agreed / that she was sure / to win the crown / again this year.

8. They all ate / fresh watermelon / from the garden.

Harcourt

Miss Owl's Secret

Circle and write the word that makes the sentence tell about the picture.

1. Mom said: "Let's get our stuff. I will

   _____ you to the park."

   tackle   tag   take

2. Jake got his _____.

   snack   skates   sakes

3. Pam packed some sandwiches, milk,

   and _____.

   grab   gave   grapes

4. The park had a _____.

   lake   last   lamp

5. Jake rested in the _____.

   shack   sad   shade

6. Mom _____ some

   ate   at   ask

   grapes and a sandwich.

7. Then Mom said, "Now we have to go.

   It is getting _____."

   lake   late   lap

Harcourt

Miss Owl's Secret

Choose the word from the box that best completes each sentence. Write it on the line.

messy	crown	watermelon	night	dark

1. Miss Owl grew this _____ in her garden.

2. In the beginning, Miss Owl's garden was _____.

3. The animals worked in the garden at _____.

4. The winner of the contest would get a _____.

5. Miss Owl can see in the _____.

Write why Miss Owl's friends wanted to help her by cleaning the garden.

_____

_____

_____

_____

Harcourt

Predict Outcomes

Read the story. Look for clues that help you predict what will happen at the end. Write your prediction and three clues that helped you.

Miss Gale's birthday was soon. Her class wanted to surprise her. At recess one day, they made plans. They knew she loved homemade things. She really liked drawings. The only way to keep it a surprise was to make a gift at recess. Michael said he would bring crayons. Mindy said she would bring art paper.

Predicted Outcome:
_____
_____

Clue:	**Clue:**	**Clue:**

Fluency Builder

boring	game	Rose
ducked	fish	Duke
sense	want	close
suppose	play	doze
tractor	doesn't	Jerome
	someone	froze
	starts	dunes
	once	

1. Rose and Jerome / played a fishing game / on the porch.

2. Jerome did not want / to play / because the game / was boring.

3. I suppose / Rose doesn't like it / when Jerome starts / to doze.

4. There was / someone standing / by the dunes.

5. Jerome froze / and ducked down / next to Duke.

6. Once, / the farmer let / the children sit / on his tractor.

7. It did not make sense / to throw back / all the fish.

8. They walked / to the store / before it could close.

Name _____

The Not-So-Boring Night

Circle and write the word that makes the sentence tell about the picture.

1. Last summer, Jane rode a

   _____ on a camping trip.

   mug   mule   mop

2. Jane, Mom, and Dad rode up a

   _____ to a lake.

   slope   cube   stop

3. Jane used a _____

   cute   pot   pole

   to catch some fish.

4. Her dad found a red _____.

   run   rose   rock

5. The rose made his _____ itch.

   not   nose   note

6. Mom dug a _____

   hot   hole   hug

   and put some stones around it.

7. Jane saw funny shapes in the

   _____.

   mule   small   smoke

8. When it got dark, the stars _____

   shone   spoke   song

   down on the camp.

Name _____

The Not-So-Boring Night

These events are from "The Not-So-Boring Night." They are out of order. Put a number in front of each one to show the right order.

_____ The farmer was throwing back the fish he got.

_____ Jerome said he liked the fishing game.

_____ Duke and Jerome went for a walk.

_____ Rose woke Jerome up.

Now write each event in the order it happened. Put each one next to an X. Then write other story events in order on the blank lines.

_____

 _____

 _____

_____

 _____

 _____

Cause and Effect

Read the story.

The Boring Day

It was raining hard, and I could not go outside. I was bored. I could not play cards, because my sister Lynn did not want to play cards. She was baking a cake. When the cake was done, we could not eat it. Our dog ate the whole thing!

Write three causes and three effects from the story.

Cause	Effect

Harcourt

Fluency Builder

captured	hat	time
imagination	over	fine
manners	says	like
matador	train	tied
plains	my	lined
relax	were	
vacation	new	
	find	

1. On my vacation, / I met a matador.

2. In my imagination, / I made up a train / that rode / over the plains.

3. Don't let your imagination be captured— / relax, / let it rest.

4. My aunt says / that my manners / are fine.

5. We tied horns / on my hat.

6. There were / cowboys lined up / by the barbed wire.

7. It is time / for the matador / to find a new job.

8. He would like / to be a farmer.

Name_____

The Matador and Me

Write the word that best completes each sentence.

hike	kite	pies	stripes	tie	shines	rides

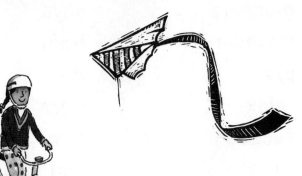

1. Todd likes to play with his

_____.

2. Jane _____

her bike to the lake.

3. I see nine _____

in the kitchen.

4. Tim and Mike went for a

_____ up a hill.

5. Dom stops to _____

his shoelaces.

6. Dave wore a shirt with black

_____.

7. The sun _____

on the vines.

Harcourt

The Matador and Me

Complete the puzzle using the words in the box. The answer for 2 Down has been done for you.

| parents | cowboys | aunt | train | instead | clothes |

Across

3. Matadors wear _____ that glitter and shine.

5. The girl's _____ think she has a big imagination.

7. The girl takes a _____ out west.

Down

1. The _____ howled when the matador fell down.

2. The big kid was dressed like a _____.

4. The matador wants to be a farmer _____.

6. The girl's _____ has a ranch on the plains.

2 Down: matador

Write about your favorite part of the story. Use as many words from the box as you can.

_____

_____

_____

Cause and Effect

Read the story.

My Summer Vacation

I loved my summer vacation because I met a matador. The matador showed me how he used a red cape to fight a bull. I did not have a red cape, so I used a blue one. "Bulls will not charge at blue capes," said the matador. Then he gave me a red cape to use.

Write three causes and three effects from the story.

Cause	Effect

Harcourt

Fluency Builder

details	feed	Neal
disappoint	comes	seal
forcibly	really	beach
information	full	meet
oceans	well	each
stroke		teaches
		seems
		real
		sleek

1. Neal meets / the seal / each weekend / on the beach.

2. Each time / they meet, / Mr. Whiskers teaches Neal / many details about seals.

3. He uses / his flippers forcibly / to reach / his top speed.

4. Oceans are full / of lots of animals / who feed on fish.

5. It seems / like the seal / talks to Neal, / but he really / does not.

6. Neal will stroke / Mr. Whiskers's back / for doing so well.

7. When Mr. Whiskers comes out / of the water, / he is so sleek!

8. Neal is disappointed / that his parents / do not think / Mr. Whiskers is real.

Harcourt

Mr. Whiskers

Fill in the oval in front of the sentence that tells about the picture best.

1 ◯ The cat is sleeping.
   ◯ Chen is eating beets.
   ◯ Chen is feeding her pet.

2 ◯ Fred and Kent have no sheets.
   ◯ I see three beds.
   ◯ Fred is dreaming of sheep.

3 ◯ Tom is sleeping on the beach.
   ◯ A seal is swimming in the deep sea.
   ◯ Meg has sneakers on her feet.

4 ◯ The sheep are near a tree.
   ◯ I see three sheep and a bee.
   ◯ The sheep are eating beans.

5 ◯ Ron is feeding the birds.
   ◯ Three cats are in a tree.
   ◯ Three birds in a tree want to eat.

6 ◯ I see bees in that tree.
   ◯ There is one leaf left on that tree.
   ◯ The leaf fell in the street.

Harcourt

Name _____

Mr. Whiskers

Neal tells a lot about Mr. Whiskers. Write *first*, *next*, or *last* under each picture to show when Neal tells about each thing.

_____ _____ _____

Complete each sentence so it tells about the story. Choose from the words in dark type.

1. Neal and Mr. Whiskers are _____ friends.

sad   sorry   dear

2. Sometimes Mr. Whiskers meets Neal at

the _____.

pond   beach   deck

3. Mr. Whiskers has made friends with big

_____.

whales   cats   shells

4. Mr. Whiskers lives in the _____.

water   forest   barn

5. Mr. Whiskers swims fast and far without getting

_____.

home   hungry   lost

Harcourt

Name _____

Make Inferences

Read the story. Then fill in the chart to make inferences.

Ms. Green

My name is Carla. This is Ms. Green, my turtle friend. I live in a house. Ms. Green lives in a pond. Ms. Green likes to eat flies, so I always bring her some for breakfast. Then Ms. Green teaches me about all the animals in the pond. My parents have never seen Ms. Green. I don't think my parents believe me when I talk about all the things Ms. Green tells me.

Clues from the Story	What We Know	Inference
Carla feeds Ms. Green	People who have pets should take good care of them.	_____ _____
Carla's parents have never seen Ms. Green	Turtles do not talk.	_____ _____ _____ _____ _____

Harcourt

Fluency Builder

admired	not	Jules
fussed	after	fruit
haze	bed	tune
mimicked	made	flute
notice	bag	Sue
pale	play	clue
	you	blue

1. Jules was / the first to notice / that Mrs. Lee / was not at home.

2. There was a haze / the morning / after the rainstorm.

3. The nurse fussed / with the blue sheets / on the bed.

4. Mrs. Lee looked / a little pale.

5. The children had made / drawings for Mrs. Lee.

6. Jules mimicked Sue / playing a tune / on the flute.

7. The tape played / the sound / of fruit dropping / into a bag.

8. Jules gave / Mrs. Lee the clue, / "It is something / you can eat."

Harcourt

Sounds All Around

Write the word from the box that best completes each sentence.

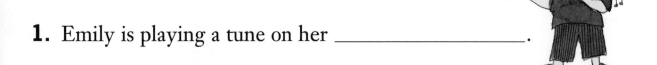

| bluebird | flute | glue | fruit | suit | ruler |

1. Emily is playing a tune on her _____ .

2. I see _____ in that basket.

3. The _____ sings for Sue.

4. Sam has on a black _____ .

5. The _____ helps Marta draw a line.

6. Gunther uses _____ to make a model plane.

Harcourt

Sounds All Around

These events are from "Sounds All Around." They are out of order. Put a number in front of each one to show the right order.

_____ Mr. Jones draws on the sidewalk.

_____ Jules thinks of a plan.

_____ Jules plays a tape for Mrs. Lee.

_____ The rain makes a mess of the chalk drawings.

Now write each event next to an X in the order it happened. Fill in the other lines by telling what else happened in the story.

_____

_____

[X] _____

[X] _____

[X] _____

_____

[X] _____

_____

Harcourt

Antonyms

Read the story. Then write an antonym, a word with an opposite meaning, for the words in the chart.

Sounds on My Street

There are a lot of nice sounds on my street. I hear children laughing. I hear birds singing a cheerful song. Sometimes I hear the ice cream truck playing its happy tune. Once in a while, there are loud sounds on my street. Sometimes I hear dump trucks. Sometimes I hear thunder from up in the sky.

Word from Story:	Antonym:
nice	_____
laughing	_____
cheerful	_____
happy	_____
loud	_____
up	_____

Harcourt

Fluency Builder

flippers	sun	bay
hatch	out	may
miserable	their	plain
slippery	these	wait
waddled	would	lay
horizon	where	play
	little	raise

1. The sun sits low / on the horizon.

2. Little blue penguins / waddled out of the bay.

3. The penguins may wave / their flippers / to greet their mate.

4. Most penguins live / where they can play / on slippery ice slides.

5. These birds / would be miserable / where it is always cold.

6. In the summer / they lay / their eggs / and raise their chicks.

7. They wait / about one month / for their eggs / to hatch.

8. The chicks are covered / with plain, / dark down.

Harcourt

Little Blue Penguins

Read the story, and circle all the words with *ai* or *ay*.

One day Gail, her dad, and her dog Brain went for a hike. Brain started to bark. "Brain, are you barking at the snail on that log?" Gail asked. Brain barked some more. "Are you barking at the jay in that

tree?" she asked. Brain barked some more. "Are you barking at the ball on the trail?" Brain wagged his tail. Gail said, "I see! You want to play with that ball. Let's go!"

Choose from the words you circled to finish each sentence.

1. _____ is the name of Gail's dog.

2. Gail asks Brain if he is barking at a _____ on a log.

3. Gail asks Brain if he is barking at a _____ in a tree.

4. Brain is barking at a ball on the _____.

5. Gail knows this after Brain wags his _____.

6. Gail knows Brain wants to _____ with the ball.

Harcourt

Little Blue Penguins

Complete the sentences with words from the box to tell what happens in "Little Blue Penguins."

flippers	eggs	underground nests
krill	Antarctica	smallest

Little blue penguins live in _____.

Tunnels keep their _____ safe.

Little blue penguins are the _____ penguins.

Little blue penguins use their wings as _____.

Little blue penguins do not live in _____.

Little blue penguins eat sea animals called _____.

Write what you liked best about little blue penguins.

_____

_____

Harcourt

Fact and Fiction

**Read the story. Then use the story
to fill in two details that are facts
and two details that are fiction. Then
tell how you made your choices.**

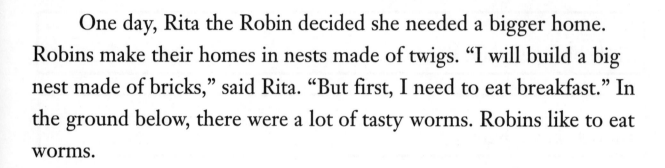

Rita the Robin

One day, Rita the Robin decided she needed a bigger home.
Robins make their homes in nests made of twigs. "I will build a big
nest made of bricks," said Rita. "But first, I need to eat breakfast." In
the ground below, there were a lot of tasty worms. Robins like to eat
worms.

Fact: _____	Fiction: _____
_____	_____
Fact: _____	Fiction: _____
_____	_____
How I Know: _____	How I Know: _____
_____	_____
_____	_____

Harcourt

Fluency Builder

caused	day	Jo
clasp	over	shiny
confused	find	we
cornered	because	secret
objects	snow	gold
removes	day	
typical	look	
	your	

1. A snow day is not / a typical day / for Lee and Jo.

2. What caused / the blocks / to be knocked over?

3. They look for clues / to find the missing objects.

4. Mom is confused / because the clasp / on her key ring / is broken.

5. A shiny gold key / will be easy / to spot.

6. We will remove / the lumps / from your bed, / Wags.

7. They have / Wags cornered.

8. Does Wags have / a secret hiding place / of his own?

Harcourt

A Secret Place

Read the story.

Di sells watches and clocks. This morning, she sold a clock.

At lunchtime, she sold a gold watch.

At six, it was time to go. It was cold outside. Di put on a coat.

Di closed the blinds. Then she went home.

Write the word that best completes each sentence.

1. _____ works in a store.

    Di   Coco   Matt

2. First, she _____ a clock.

    song   sold   so

3. Then _____ sold a gold watch.

    I   she   we

4. She put on a coat because it was _____.

    cold   clock   fold

5. At six, she closed the _____.

    bins   grinds   blinds

Name _____

A Secret Place

Complete the chart with words from the box to tell what happened in "A Secret Place."

small	missing	chief	key	shiny	clues

A toy car and some blocks were _____.

A _____ was lost, too.

Mom said, "You need to look for _____."

Jo was the _____ and Lee was the helper.

Lee said a _____ gold key would be easy to spot.

Wags was a _____ dog, but he was very smart.

Answer these questions to tell about the rest of the story.

1. What were the missing things? _____

_____

2. Who had the missing things? _____

3. Who found the missing things? _____

4. Think of another way the family could have found the missing

things. Write it here. _____

_____

Harcourt

Narrative Elements

Read the story and copy the narrative elements in the correct boxes.

Will had to give his dog a bath. First, he got some soap. Then he put water in the tub. Will got the dog and put him in the tub. At last, the dog was clean and beautiful.

Will put the dog in the tub.

The dog needed a bath.

Will got soap.

The bathroom

Will

The dog

Will put water in the tub.

Setting	Problem
_____ _____	_____ _____

Characters	Events
_____ _____	_____ _____

How Problem is Solved
_____   _____

Harcourt

Fluency Builder

addresses	started	sky
clerk	know	Myles
grown	think	Clyde
honor	tried	Pryor
pour	was	fly
route	into	July
	play	spy

1. Myles lives / in the sky-blue house / next to Ms. Pryor, / the town clerk.

2. In July / mail started / to pour / into the children's mailboxes.

3. Who would know / all of their addresses?

4. Myles tried / to think / like a spy.

5. The mail was not coming / on the mail route.

6. A grown person / was sneaking / the mail / into the mailboxes.

7. Myles planned / a birthday party / in honor / of Mr. Clyde.

8. They will play games / and fly kites!

Harcourt

Hello from Here

Write the word that completes each sentence best.

by	fly	dry	Why	tries	sky	cries	shy

1. Little Robin sees birds up in the _____.

2. He wants to _____ in the sky, too.

3. _____ is flying so hard?

4. Little Robin feels a little bit _____.

5. Now he is wet, but he wants to be _____.

6. Little Robin _____ hard.

7. He _____ to fly again.

8. Now Little Robin can fly all _____ himself!

Harcourt

Name _____

Hello from Here

**Write a word to complete the sentences about the story.
Choose from the words in dark type.**

1. Mr. Clyde had no _____.

            mailbox   car   grandchildren

2. Mr. Clyde gave the kids a big _____.

              surprise   cake   party

3. One boy hid by a _____ to find out who sent
the postcards. **car   mailbox   house**

4. He saw Mr. Clyde coming up the _____.

              street   steps   ramp

5. Mr. Clyde had waited _____ to try sky diving.

         what   days   years

6. The kids had a _____ for Mr. Clyde.

      card   kite   party

Write answers to these questions.

7. What clue did the boy use to find out who was sending the cards?

_____

8. Why did the boy send cards to the kids on his street?

_____

Compare and Contrast

Read the stories. Then fill in the diagram to show how the stories are alike and different.

Story 1

The kittens were in their basket. Their mother was off looking for food. One kitten saw some yarn on the floor. He wanted to get it. He left the basket. His sisters came, too. They played with the ball of yarn for a long time. When their mother came back, they were all asleep in the basket. They had played hard.

Story 2

Jason was in his yard. He was playing ball. He hit the ball with his bat. The ball went up in the sky. His mother came to catch it. Jason and his mother played together for a long time. They had a lot of fun. When they were done, Jason went to sleep. It had been a long day.

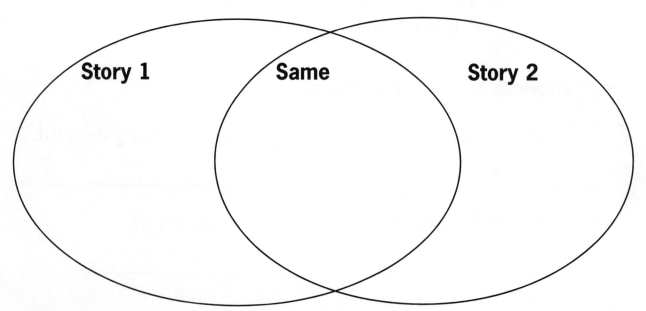

Story 1   Same   Story 2

Harcourt

Fluency Builder

appeared	liked	Dwight
conductor	find	right
created	would	fright
imitated	side	night
rhythm	dad	high
startled	game	delighted
	new	
	his	

1. Dwight liked to find / new ways / to make his rhythm / sound better.

2. He would try / to get / just the right sound.

3. The loud sound / startled the children nearby.

4. Linda appeared / by his side / and said, / "You gave me / such a fright!"

5. Jon imitated / a trumpet player.

6. Dwight's dad created / a steel drum / in his workshop.

7. The conductor lifted his arms high, / and Dwight / delighted the crowd.

8. He played / "The Star-Spangled Banner" / at the game Saturday night.

Harcourt

Name _____

The Music Maker

Write the word that makes the sentence tell about the picture.

1. "Let's take a walk to the _____,"
said Mom.   **nightshirt   nighttime   lighthouse**

2. "How will we find the path at _____?"
asked Tim.   **fight   night   tight**

3. "We will use a _____," Mom
replied.   **flashlight   lightning   night**

4. The lighthouse sits _____ up on a cliff.
    sight   hide   high

5. It has a big _____ at the top.
    flight   light   like

6. The light is very _____.
    bride   might   bright

7. The light shows ships the _____ way
to go.   **ride   right   rind**

8. Ann tells her mom, "I _____ work
there someday."   **might   night   light**

Harcourt

The Music Maker

Write a word on each line. Complete the story strip to show the order of events in "The Music Maker."

Dwight put rubber bands on his _____ . **sticks drum**	First, Dwight drummed on his _____ . **bucket boxes**	Next, Dwight drummed on the _____ . **bucket basket**
When Dwight drummed on a _____ , **garbage can box** he gave his friends a fright.	Dwight planned to play a tune at the _____ **game show** on Saturday.	Linda said, "You can't play a _____ **rhythm tune** with a drum."
Dwight _____ , **answered danced** "Yes, I can."	Dwight's dad _____ **made bought** steel drums.	When he put the heated can in water, _____ **drops clouds** of steam came up.

Multiple-meaning Words

A **multiple-meaning word** has more than one meaning. Read the words around it to find out which meaning makes sense.

Read the sentences. Decide which meaning is correct.

1. I will **plant** this tree.

   a. a green, growing thing

   b. to put into the ground

2. I will keep the **flies** off it.

   a. moves through the air

   b. small, black bugs

3. I will keep the **cold** off it.

   a. the opposite of heat

   b. a runny nose

4. I will give it to my dad as a **present**.

   a. gift

   b. right now

Harcourt

Fluency Builder

dappled	your	shiny
exhibitions	would	pony
landscape	work	risky
business	falls	dirty
ranch	have	dusty
thousands	their	silly
	horses	field

1. Would you trade / your shiny bike / for a dappled pony?

2. The rodeo is / an exhibition / of style and skill.

3. Many riders / in small rodeos / work on a ranch.

4. If a cowboy falls off of a bronco, / then he'll see the landscape / up close.

5. Ropers have to practice / their skill / thousands of times.

6. Riding a bull / is a risky business.

7. Silly clowns have / dirty, / dusty, / and dangerous work.

8. At the end of the rodeo, / horses can go out / to the field and graze.

Name _____

Rodeo!

Complete each sentence with a word from the box.

chilly	sleepy	puppies	dirty
Fluffy	family	hungry	happy

1. Penny asks, "Mom, may I have

   one of the _____?"

2. Mom asks, "Penny, will you feed the

   puppy when he is _____?"

3. "Will you wash the puppy when

   he is _____?"

4. "Will you walk the puppy when it

   is _____ outside?"

5. "Will you play with the puppy at night

   when you are _____?"

6. Penny says, "Yes, Mom. The puppy will

   be very _____ with me."

7. Mom says, "Now the puppy is a part of our

   _____. What will you call him?"

8. Penny says, "I will call him

   _____!"

Harcourt

Rodeo!

Complete the puzzle with words from the box.

horse	practice	rope	ride	birthday	style

Across

1. Riding well takes a lot of ___ .

4. A cowboy must ___ a bucking horse for 8 seconds.

5. A cowgirl's ___ helps her keep her rope tight.

6. ___ is not needed to ride a bull.

Down

2. A cowgirl may have thrown her ___ thousands of times.

3. July 4 is the rodeo's ___ .

Write the completed clues on the lines below.

_____

_____

_____

_____

_____

_____

Harcourt

Summarize/Restate

Read the paragraph.

Sedona has many great things to see. People come to see the famous red rocks. There are lots of places to hike. Many people go to Slide Rock to play in the water. People also come to hear jazz. You can also ride in a hot-air balloon. Sedona has lots of art exhibitions, too.

Fill in the web.

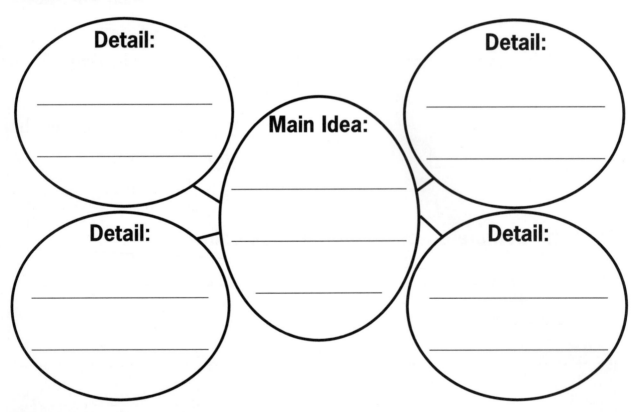

Detail: _____

Detail: _____

Main Idea: _____

Detail: _____

Detail: _____

Use your web to write a summary on the lines below.

_____

_____

Harcourt

Fluency Builder

celebrations	with	roads
develop	Grandma	blowing
furious	all	showed
graceful	trucks	loaf
grocery store	store	grow
students	cake	glowed
	lion	
	when	

1. Chinese characters are made / with graceful brush strokes.

2. Of all the celebrations, / the Chinese New Year / is Grandma's favorite.

3. Chinatown's roads were noisy / with delivery trucks / and blowing horns.

4. Grandma showed Jimmy / how to shop for fruit / at the grocery store.

5. At the bakery / they bought a loaf, / sweets, / and a New Year's cake.

6. The kung fu students / were carrying / a furious-looking lion mask.

7. Grandma told Jimmy / that melon will help you / develop and grow.

8. Jimmy glowed / with happiness / when his parents arrived.

Harcourt

Happy New Year!

Fill in the oval in front of the sentence that tells about the picture.

1 ⬭ Ron owns a white coat.
⬭ Ron rows a boat.
⬭ Ron is throwing a snowball.

2 ⬭ The plant is slow to grow.
⬭ Joan will eat some toast.
⬭ I see a flower in the snow.

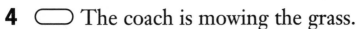

3 ⬭ The bowl is round.
⬭ Tam shows Rick her new soap.
⬭ Rick knows Tam owns a ball.

4 ⬭ The coach is mowing the grass.
⬭ A girl throws the coat.
⬭ Joan has scored a goal.

5 ⬭ The log floats on a road.
⬭ Four toads sit in a row.
⬭ I see three toads and a goat.

6 ⬭ The truck can tow a boat.
⬭ A crow is on the truck.
⬭ Joan and Bob will tow a bowl.

Happy New Year!

These events are from the story "Happy New Year!" They are out of order. Put a number in front of each one to show the right order.

___ Jimmy and Grandma went shopping.

___ Jimmy's mother and father came back early.

___ Jimmy and Grandma cleaned the apartment.

___ The family members began to arrive.

Answer these questions to tell about the rest of the story.

1. What did Jimmy and Grandma hang up in the apartment?

_____

2. What did Jimmy and Grandma buy when they went shopping?

_____

3. What did the kung fu students have?

_____

4. Why did Grandma set out chairs for Jimmy's parents?

_____

_____

Harcourt

Name _____

Details

Read the paragraph.

    Long ago in China there was a monster. Its name was
Nian. He liked to scare people. The people did not like him.
"Go pick on other monsters," they cried. Nian went away for
a year. Then he came back. Some children were using firecrackers. BANG! The noise scared Nian away. Now people
always use firecrackers on Chinese New Year. They keep Nian
away.

Write four details from the paragraph that tell about Nian.

1. Detail _____

2. Detail _____

3. Detail _____

4. Detail _____

Harcourt

Name _____

Fluency Builder

flock	wanted	look
glide	bird	book
harbor	over	cook
soared	rain	soon
swooping	down	
clouds	across	
window	would	
everyone	world	

1. Luke wanted / to glide / like a bird.

2. In his imagination / he soared / over the rain clouds.

3. June would join / a flock of birds / down at the harbor.

4. She would go swooping / across the wide / blue sea.

5. Soon / everyone would know / how to fly.

6. Sally would look / in her grandma's window.

7. Grandma would cook Sally / the best meal / in the world.

8. Sally would read / from her book / until her grandma / fell asleep.

Name _____

If I Could Fly

Fill in the oval in front of the sentence that tells about the picture.

1 ◯ Sue put the ball in the pool.
   ◯ The ball went in the hoop.
   ◯ Sue stood on the book.

2 ◯ The robin makes a loop.
   ◯ The bird is at the zoo.
   ◯ The bird flies in front of the moon.

3 ◯ Nate shook the fruit down.
   ◯ Nate waded in the brook.
   ◯ Nate stood on a stool.

4 ◯ Lew gives the book to Sue.
   ◯ Lew has a new cookbook.
   ◯ Lew likes his new boots.

5 ◯ My boots are in that room.
   ◯ We will go to the pool soon.
   ◯ There is a toolbox on the roof.

6 ◯ Dan looks for his blue shoe.
   ◯ He cooks a good stew.
   ◯ The boy hooks a fish in the brook.

Harcourt

If I Could Fly

Read the clues. Then complete the puzzle with words from the box.

country	adventure	grandma	city	buildings	people

Across

3. Luke wanted to look into the windows of _____.

6. June said she wanted to go to a new _____.

Down

1. Luke wanted to go to a _____.

2. Luke told his friends he would have the best _____.

4. Sally said she wanted to visit her _____.

5. June said she wanted to find a place where _____ play all the time.

On another sheet of paper, write the completed clues. Write a number in front of each sentence to show the order of events in the story.

Make Inferences

Read the story. Then use clues from the story and what you know to make inferences about the girl in the story.

If No One Could See Me

My name is Sara. I like to play make-believe. Sometimes I pretend that no one can see me. If no one could see me, I would help people who were in trouble. For example, I would pick people up after they fell. They would be so surprised! Then I would let them see me, and we would laugh.

Story Clue: Sara likes to play make-believe.

What I Know: _____

_____

My Inference: _____

Story Clue: Sara would help people who were in trouble.

What I Know: _____

_____

My Inference: _____

Harcourt

Fluency Builder

connects	made	orange
distance	world	German
features	round	Germany
mapmaker	and	pages
peel	went	change
	trip	game
	between	
	through	
	your	

1. The mapmaker made / a globe round / to be a model / of the world.

2. If you could peel the globe / like an orange / and lay the strips flat, / then you would have / a world map.

3. A globe shows / land and water features.

4. The Atlantic Ocean connects / the continents / of South America / and Africa.

5. Pretend you went / on a trip / to a German village.

6. What is the distance / between your home / and Germany?

7. Look through the pages / of books / to find the answers.

8. How can you change / the rules of the game / to make it / even more fun?

Harcourt

Name _____

Map Games

Read this story. Circle the words that have the g sound you hear in *gem*.

Gerry and Ginny

Gerry thinks this is a good day to be outside. He walks past the hedge to the edge of the river. He sits under a giant tree. Gerry looks at the sky. He feels a gentle wind.

Ginny thinks this is a good day to be inside. She thinks it is going to rain. She wants to play inside. She goes to the gym to play games.

Use some of the words you circled to complete each sentence.

1. Gerry sits by the _____ of the river.

2. He is near a _____ tree.

3. There is a _____ wind.

4. _____ goes inside.

5. She wants to play games in the _____.

108 Grade 2 • Lesson 27/Phonics: /j/g, dge

Harcourt

Name _____

Map Games

Circle the word that best completes each sentence. Write it on the line.

1. You can use a

_____

ball   orange   globe

to play map games.

2. A globe shows land and water

_____.

continents features villages

3. The Atlantic Ocean

_____

connects   peels   distances

the continents of South America and Africa.

4. You can guess the

_____

feature   map   distance

from one place on the globe to another.

5. A globe is like a round _____.

village   continent   map

On the lines below, write what you learned from the story.

_____

_____

_____

Locate Information

Read the table of contents for an atlas. Then use the table of contents to answer the questions.

My Atlas
Table of Contents

1. On which page would you find information about the

   Mississippi River in North America? _____

2. Where would you find a picture of the continent of Africa?

   _____

3. Which pages would help you compare and contrast the

   mountain ranges of North America and Africa?

   _____

4. Which page might tell you about where people work in Africa?

   _____

Harcourt

Fluency Builder

cassette	you	joy
companions	want	point
luggage	ask	noise
relatives	help	join
sturdy	around	avoid
	too	toys
	lot	boys
	with	

1. Make a point / to call your relatives / before you visit.

2. You might want to ask / if a companion / can join you.

3. Pack sturdy clothes / and toys / in your luggage.

4. The boys offer to help / with the chores / around the house.

5. Avoid turning / your cassette player / too high.

6. Don't make / a lot of noise.

7. Make a point / of writing / a thank-you note.

8. Your relatives will remember / your visit / with joy!

Harcourt

When You Visit Relatives

Complete each sentence so it tells about the picture.

1. Roy is a tall _____.

oil   boy   bee

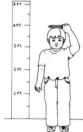

2. I put the _____ away.

coin   boy   join

3. The water starts to _____.

point   boil   boat

4. Joy will _____ the softball team.

coil   jog   join

5. I plant seeds in the _____.

soil   seal   spoil

6. This _____ train is fun.

join   top   toy

7. That bird makes a lot of _____.

boys   coins   noise

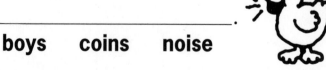

Harcourt

When You Visit Relatives

Write *beginning*, *middle*, or *end* under each picture to show the order of events in "When You Visit Relatives."

Dear Relatives,
Thank you
for everything.
Love,
Ernest

See you soon!

_____   _____   _____

Now use the words in the gray boxes to answer the questions.

Beginning	relatives travel

What does Ernest want to do? _____

_____

Middle	bicycle weather forgets

What is Ernest's trip like? _____

_____

What happens at his relatives' house?   **helps   broke**

_____

End	note relatives

What does Ernest remember to do at the end of his visit?

_____

Author's Purpose

Write the author's purpose. Write three clues that helped you tell the author's purpose.

Here Comes Company!

If you want to get ready for company, you should give yourself lots of time. First, you should clean your room. Then, you can prepare some nice snacks. Put the toys and the games you will want to play with your company in a neat pile. After that, you may want to take a bath and put on some nice clothes. Finally, wait for the doorbell to ring!

Author's Purpose: _____
Clue: _____   _____
Clue: _____   _____
Clue: _____   _____

Harcourt

Fluency Builder

Name _____

cozy	rain	caused
drifted	cave	crawled
fleet	past	hawk
launched	find	dawn
looming	would	paused
realized	were	saw
	from	yawned

1. Zelda yawned / when she reached / her cozy cave.

2. The rain caused / the water / to rise / in the cave.

3. Zelda crawled out / onto the ledge.

4. A bottle drifted past / in the waves.

5. Zelda realized / she would have / to find / a new home.

6. Dark clouds were looming / when Zelda launched herself / from the ledge.

7. Zelda flew / like a hawk / over a fleet / of sailboats.

8. Zelda paused / at dawn / when she saw / sand below.

Harcourt

Zelda Moves to the Desert

Read the sentences, then do what they tell you.

1. Do you see the baby crawling? Color his shirt yellow.
2. Can you find the hawk? Draw a tree for it to perch on.
3. Color the lawn green.
4. Do you see someone yawning? Color her shirt blue.
5. Find the fawn and circle it. Color it brown.
6. Shauna has pasta with sauce for lunch. Color the sauce red.
7. Draw some clouds in the sky.
8. Can you see the dog? Color him black with white paws.

Circle the words with the vowel sound you hear in _saw_.

Harcourt

Name _____

Zelda Moves to the Desert

Complete the flowchart with words from the box to tell what happens in "Zelda Moves to the Desert."

waves	bottle	sank	flooded	sail	mice

Zelda left her home because it _____.

The heavy rain made _____ in the water.

A rock _____ far down in the water. Zelda knew it was deep.

Zelda saw a _____ float by.

Some _____ floated by in a bowl.

They lost the _____ for their boat.

Answer these questions to tell about the rest of the story.

1. Where did Zelda fly first? _____

2. Was that a good home for her? Explain your answer. _____

_____

3. Where did Zelda fly next? _____

4. Where did Zelda find her new home? _____

_____

Harcourt

Homophones

Homophones are words that sound alike but are not spelled alike. Read the story and underline the homophones. Write the meaning of each homophone.

A New Home

Marty loved to sail on the sea. "I want
to buy a new home," said Marty. He walked by a store. A sign in the window said Cozy Homes for Sale. "Hi," said Marty to the owner of the store. "I see you have homes for sale. Do you have a houseboat?" "Yes we do," said the owner. "That's the house for me!" said Marty.

sail	sale
sea	see
buy	by

Fluency Builder

feat	who	city
heroine	her	celebrate
hospitality	came	cities
refused	from	decided
spectators	their	since
stood	around	chance
	world	center

1. Amelia Earhart / was a heroine / who accomplished / a great feat.

2. Amelia refused / to sit at home / in the city.

3. Soon flying became / the center / of Amelia's life.

4. Spectators came / from miles around / and stood / to celebrate Amelia's arrival.

5. Amelia thanked / the different cities / for their hospitality.

6. Amelia decided / to fly / all the way / around the world.

7. Hundreds of people / have looked / for the plane / ever since it disappeared.

8. Amelia took a chance / to fulfill her dreams.

Harcourt

An Amazing Feat

Read the story. Circle the words that have the c sound you hear in *city*.

The Race

Today is the bicycle race in Cedar City. The race goes in a big circle around Cash Park. Kim finds a space at the starting line. He ties his shoelaces. He puts on his nice new helmet. Then the race begins. The wind on Kim's face is cool. After the race, Kim drinks some juice. He didn't win, but he still celebrates with his mom and dad.

Choose from the words you circled to complete each sentence.

1. There is a bicycle _____ today.

2. The race is in Cedar _____.

3. The race goes in a big _____ around the park.

4. Kim feels the wind on his _____.

5. He drinks _____ after the race.

6. He _____ with his mom and dad.

Harcourt

Name _____

An Amazing Feat

Complete the chart to tell about the story.

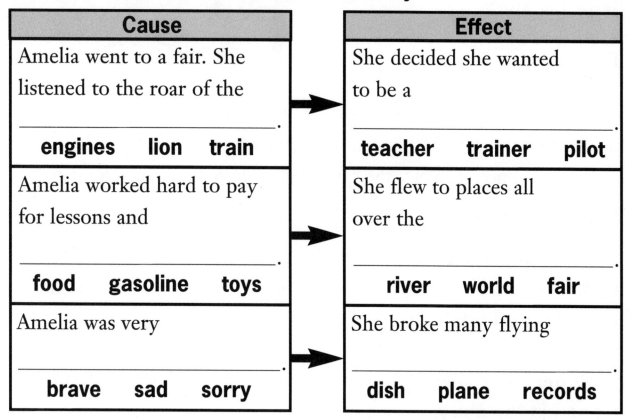

Cause	Effect
Amelia went to a fair. She listened to the roar of the _____. **engines lion train**	She decided she wanted to be a _____. **teacher trainer pilot**
Amelia worked hard to pay for lessons and _____. **food gasoline toys**	She flew to places all over the _____. **river world fair**
Amelia was very _____. **brave sad sorry**	She broke many flying _____. **dish plane records**

Answer these questions to tell about the rest of the story.

1. What brave thing did Amelia want to do when she was 40?

_____

_____

2. What was her plane filled with? _____

3. What happened to Amelia on this flight? _____

_____

4. If you could meet Amelia Earhart, what would you ask her?

_____

Harcourt

Predict Outcomes

Read the story.

The Freezing Flight

Cara put on two woolen suits. She put on a leather jacket. She needed to be warm enough. Cara was flying to the North Pole! "I hope I have enough fuel," she said. Pilots know that surprises can happen.

Cara flew many miles north. It began to snow hard. She could not see out the plane's tiny window. Suddenly, she heard a strange sound. It was inside the plane.

Fill in the story clues, what you know, and what you predict will happen in the story.

Story Clues	What I Know	My Prediction

Harcourt